BIBLE STORIES to Live by

Volume One: Stories 1-46

46 Exciting Stories
from the
OLD TESTAMENT

V. Gilbert Beers
& Ronald A. Beers

Here's Life Publishers

TO PARENTS AND TEACHERS

You are part of a growing number of parents and teachers who are concerned about their children. Many are searching for a way for their children to learn "old-fashioned" moral and spiritual values such as honesty, courage, love, self-control and reverence. These time-honored values may seem old-fashioned, but they are as contemporary as today's child who is under construction, and who will become tomorrow's Christian leader.

Each story in this book focuses on one of the familiar values so important for our children. These values are seen at work in the lives of Bible-time people. Sometimes a story shows how that person failed to show love, or reverence, and why that hurt. At other times the story shows how a person showed love or reverence, and why that worked.

Questions help your child understand how each moral or spiritual value can be applied today in his or her own life.

In the back you will find an alphabetical guide to the moral and spiritual values taught in this book.

BIBLE STORIES TO LIVE BY: VOLUME 1
The Old Testament

Illustrations by Reint De Jonge

Two-volume edition published 1990 by
HERE'S LIFE PUBLISHERS, INC.
P. O. Box 1576
San Bernardino, CA 92402

ISBN 0-89840-302-2
© 1983, V. Gilbert Beers and Ronald A. Beers

Adapted from:**The Kleuterbijbel**
Originally published by: Boekencentrum B.V.
                        Scheveningseweg 72
                        25717 KX's-Gravenhage
                        The Netherlands

Contents

God Makes a Wonderful World

A Story about ORDERLINESS

In the beginning, there was nothing... nothing but God. No world had been made, no sun, moon, or stars. There were no birds or animals or plants or trees. Instead, there was nothing but darkness and empty space.

But God had a wonderful plan. He called it creation. God would fill the dark empty spaces with beautiful things. He would make these beautiful things from nothing.

At the right time, God began His wonderful work. "Let there be light!" God said. Light appeared in the dark skies and the darkness hid from it. God called the light places day and the dark places night.

"Let there be a sky above and an earth below!" God said. The earth formed into a beautiful ball and the sky rose above it. A clear horizon appeared where the earth and the sky met.

"Let the waters gather together and the dry land appear," God said. The waters moved together to form the seas and the dry land appeared, with mountains and valleys and fields.

"Let grass and plants and trees grow upon the dry land," God said. The land burst forth with beautiful flowers and bushes, trees and plants. God must have smiled at the wonder of it all.

God spoke and the sun warmed the earth. He spoke and the moon appeared. One by one stars twinkled in the skies.

"Let birds and fish and animals appear," God said. The quiet skies broke forth in birdsong and the still waters sparkled with fish. Animals ran across the hills. The earth was a garden of beauty and harmony. Everything was exactly where it should be, and everything worked together exactly the way it should, like the parts of a beautiful watch. And God saw that it was good!

THINK

1. Think about the world that God made. Why do you think God made it? Why didn't it just happen? 2. The world keeps better time in its movements than the finest watch. Why didn't this just happen? 3. Think about the beautiful flowers that come from seeds. Why didn't this just happen?

LEARN

From this story you learn about God's orderliness. God put everything in the right place. When the world gets out of place, it is because we messed it up. God didn't.

DO

Draw a big circle. This is the world. Now draw in and around the circle some things that God made. Don't forget the sun, moon, stars, trees, animals, and people.

A Garden Home

A Story about HAPPINESS

The whole earth was a beautiful garden, with sights and sounds and smells blending together. God was pleased with His work. He was pleased to see how well everything worked together. But it was too wonderful to keep for Himself alone. God planned to share it with someone—someone like Himself.

One place was more beautiful than all others. God created a man, named him Adam, and put him in charge of this beautiful garden called Eden. There wasn't much for Adam to do in Eden, for everything worked together the way it should.

One day God brought each kind of animal to Adam so that he could name them. Then He put Adam in charge of the animals. Adam was glad for the animals, but something—someone—was missing. God knew who this someone was, and He knew what to do.

God put Adam to sleep and then took a rib from his side and made a woman. He brought the woman to Adam to become his wife.

Together Adam and his wife lived happily in Eden. Why shouldn't they be happy? What more could they need?

Adam and Eve not only had everything they needed, but they also had everything they wanted. Then God told them about something they could not have, something they should not want.

"You may eat anything in the Garden of Eden except one fruit," God told them. "If you eat the fruit from the tree of the knowledge of good and evil you will die."

Adam and Eve listened carefully to God. As long as they obeyed Him, they lived happily in their garden home.

THINK

1. Think about the things Adam and Eve had. What more did they need? What more should they have wanted? 2. Now think about the things you have. What more do you need? What more should you want?

LEARN

From this story, you learn about happiness. As long as Adam and Eve obeyed God, they were happy. As long as you obey God and your parents, you can be happy.

DO

Do you remember the last time you felt unhappy? Ask yourself what happened just before that. Did you disobey God or your parents? The next time you are unhappy, ask quickly if you have disobeyed.

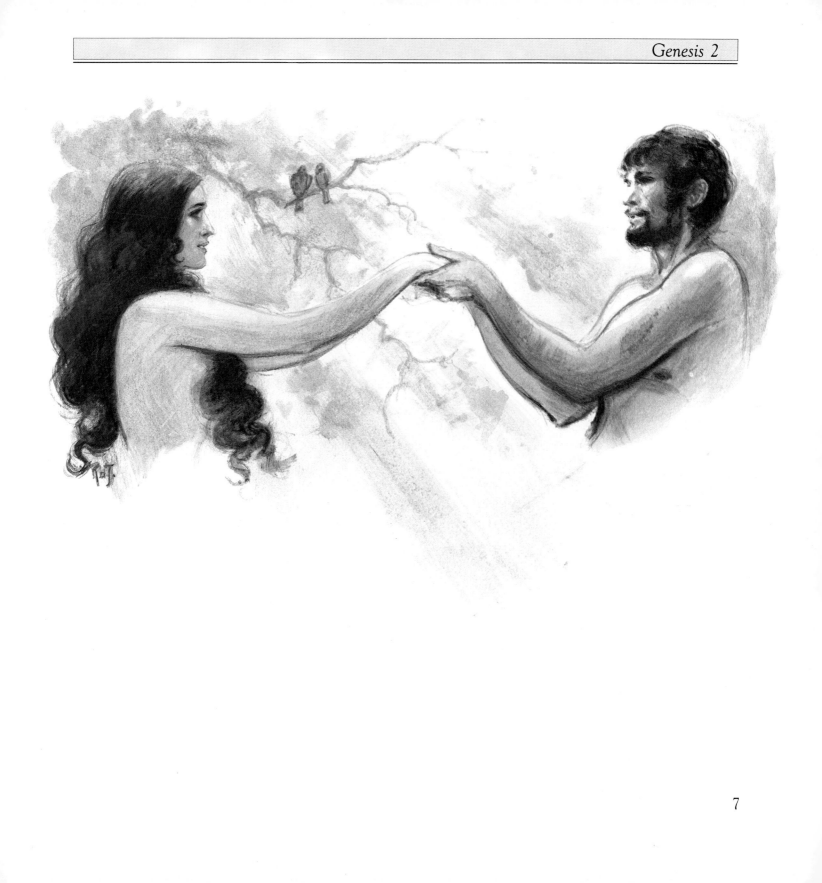

Adam and Eve Are Tempted

A Story about TEMPTATION

"Did God REALLY say that?" the serpent asked Eve. "God said we may eat anything in the garden except this fruit," Eve answered. "If we eat this, we will die."

"You won't die," Satan, the serpent said. "When you eat this fruit, you will see things you never saw before. You will know the difference between good and evil."

When Satan tempts, he tells little half truths. He was half right and half wrong. Adam and Eve would not lie down and die and be buried. But when they disobeyed God, sin would come between them and God and would keep them from being good friends with God. This kind of death is much worse than the other.

Eve listened to Satan's words. They did not seem half true. She thought they were all true. So she ate some of the fruit and gave some to Adam to eat too.

Satan's half truth was right. Adam and Eve did not lie down and die. But something died inside. They knew they had sinned against God. They knew that sin had come between them and God and had spoiled their beautiful friendship with Him. They were ashamed, so ashamed that they made fig-leaf clothes to wear and they hid from God. They did not want to see God or talk with Him. But God found them and spoke to them.

"Because you did not obey Me, you must leave the Garden of Eden," God told Adam and Eve. "You must work hard for a living. You will have sorrow and pain." Adam and Eve were sorry now that they had disobeyed God and had sinned. They were sorry that they had spoiled their friendship with God. This was worse than dying!

DO

Write two words on a piece of paper—EVE and PRAY. Next time you are tempted to do something wrong, take this paper from your pocket or book and look at it. It will remind you of the trouble Eve had when she was tempted. It will remind you to pray and ask God to help you.

THINK

1. What spoiled the friendship that Adam and Eve had with God? 2. Why did Adam and Eve eat this fruit when they already had all that they needed? 3. How have you been tempted? What were you tempted to do? Why did you think you needed this? 4. Next time you are tempted, pray!

LEARN

From this story, you learn that you are tempted to do things God does not want you to do, and these things will hurt your friendship with God.

9

Cain Kills Abel

A Story about JEALOUSY

As time passed Adam and Eve had two sons. Cain grew up and became a grain farmer. Abel grew up and became a shepherd.

These two young men were quite different. Abel pleased God but Cain did not. Both young men gave offerings to God, but they did not give the same way.

Cain saw that God rewarded Abel more than him. God was more pleased with Abel's offerings because He was more pleased with Abel and the way he lived for God. This made Cain more jealous each day.

Jealousy has a way of eating the smile from our faces and the laughter from our hearts. That's what happened to Cain. His face grew bitter and angry, showing what was in his heart.

"Why do you look that way?" God asked Cain. "If you please Me, I will accept you. If you keep on sinning, it will control you."

That is exactly what happened. One day Cain's jealousy ate too deep into his heart. While he and Abel were working in the fields, Cain, in a fit of anger, struck Abel and killed him.

Cain had lost control of himself. Jealousy took over. On that sad day, God punished Cain by sending him away from his home, his family, and from God Himself. Lonely and afraid, Cain ran, and he kept on running—running away from the terrible thing jealousy made him do, and running away from God.

THINK

1. What terrible thing did Cain do to Abel? 2. Why did he do this? 3. How did jealousy cause him to kill his brother? 4. What do you do when you are jealous? Remember Cain and Abel.

LEARN

From this story you learn how jealousy eats away at our hearts and minds and makes us do things we should not do.

DO

Are you jealous of someone now? Is someone jealous of you? Tonight before you go to bed, pray and ask God to help you or your jealous friend.

Noah and the Great Flood

A Story about OBEDIENCE

Many years passed after the time of Cain and Abel. People forgot about God and lived the way they wanted to live, not the way God wanted them to live. By the time of Noah, almost everyone was living sad, sinful lives. Only Noah and his family pleased God.

God was not pleased with Noah's wicked neighbors. He was sorry that He had made them. So God said, "I will destroy these people and their animals." Only Noah and his family would be spared.

"Make an ark, a large boat," God told Noah. "I will send a flood upon the earth. It will destroy people and animals. But you and your family will be safe in the ark."

God told Noah to bring two of each kind of animal, a male and a female, into this ark. Through them, all future animals would be born.

The ark would be as big as seventy-five houses, much longer than a football field, and as tall as a three-story building. Think of the work Noah and his sons must do to make such a boat!

Noah and his family were discouraged many times as they cut trees, sawed them into beams or boards, and hammered them into place on the ark. They wanted to quit when neighbors laughed at them for building this boat far from the ocean.

But Noah obeyed God and did all that God told him to do. For a hundred and twenty years he kept on cutting, sawing, carrying, hammering, and listening to his neighbors. He kept on obeying God, even when he wanted to quit.

But the day came when Noah and his family were glad that they had obeyed God. The rains fell and the waters roared up from the depths of the seas. For forty days and forty nights, the rain came down in torrents. All who were outside the ark were drowned. Inside the ark, Noah, his family, and the animals were safe and dry.

What a sad day that would have been if Noah had not obeyed God!

THINK

1. What would you think if God told you to build a big boat at the edge of your town? What must Noah have thought? But he did it because God said to do it. 2. What do you think when your parents ask you to do something? Do you obey without grumbling? Should you?

LEARN

From this story, you learn that it pays to obey God. It pays also to obey your parents.

DO

Pretend you are a mother or father and your pet is your child. Ask your "child" to come for dinner, or do something that will help him. Do you expect him to obey?

Noah Thanks God

A Story about PROMISES

Living on the ark was not much fun for Noah and his family. Each day they fed the animals, cleaned the stalls, and did the other chores. They could not go out into the back yard or go next door to see the neighbors. There was no back yard and there were no neighbors. There was no one else in the world and nowhere else to go.

Noah and his family could not even see outside the ark. The only window was too small and too high for them to look outside.

But Noah and his family did not complain about the chores or the other problems. They were safe and dry inside the ark. Their neighbors were not, for they were drowned in the flood.

The months passed slowly on the ark. They had time to think about the things that God had done. How thankful they were that they had believed God's promise that a flood would come. How thankful they were that they had believed God when He told them to build this boat. And how thankful they were that they had believed God's promise to save Noah and his family if they would obey Him and build the ark.

At last it was time for Noah and his family to leave the ark. A new world smiled as they stepped outside. The sun never seemed brighter or the trees and flowers more beautiful. The animals, penned up for a year inside the ark, romped and played upon the hills, and the birds soared high into the skies.

Noah and his family made an altar. They thanked God for saving them. They thanked God for keeping His promises.

God had another promise for Noah. "Never again will I destroy My people and animals with a flood over all the earth," He said. Then God sent a beautiful rainbow. It was a sign, a way to help Noah, and us, remember that God always keeps His promises.

THINK

1. What did God promise if Noah built the ark? How did God keep His promise to Noah? 2. Think what would have happened if Noah had not believed God's promise. What may have been different?

LEARN

From this story, you learn that God always keeps His promises. Since God keeps His promises, you should keep yours.

DO

Look up Romans 4:21 in your Bible. CAN God do what He promises? Now look up I Kings 8:56. WILL God do what He promises?

Abram Goes to a New Land

A Story about OBEDIENCE

Do you remember hearing about Abraham and Sarah? When they were younger, they lived in a land near Ur, and were called Abram and Sarai. The neighbors at Ur seemed like decent, well-to-do people, but they built pyramid-shaped towers, called ziggurats, where they worshipped strange gods.

God spoke to Abram and told him to go to a land far away. So Abram and his entire family left Ur and moved toward this new land. Along the way they stopped at a place called Haran, far to the north. There the family settled down and lived until Abram's father Terah died.

Then God spoke to Abram again. "Leave your home and family here at Haran, and go to a land I will show you," God told him. "In this new land you will have many children, and your descendants will become a great nation. Through you all families on earth will be blessed."

Moving to a new land and living among strange people was not easy in Abram's time. It would have been easier for Abram to stay in Haran and live the rest of his life with family and friends.

But Abram obeyed God. With Sarai, his nephew Lot, and all his possessions, Abram moved across the many miles to the land of Canaan, the land where God led him. Travel was hard, mile upon mile swaying wearily on camels, or walking across the dusty trails which were the only roads of that time.

Travel was slow, too, for Abram and his people could go no faster than the young lambs and calves of their flocks and herds. But no matter how hard, or how slowly they had to move, Abram obeyed God and went where God told him to go.

When Abram and Sarai arrived at last in Canaan, God spoke to them again. "I will give this land to your descendants," God promised. Abram believed God and built an altar, one of many he would build in Canaan. Upon this altar, Abram offered gifts to God, showing that he would obey God completely, no matter where He would lead.

THINK

1. Think how hard it was for Abram and Sarai to move to a new land. Why did they go to all this trouble? 2. Do you think Abram and Sarai were glad they obeyed God? Why? 3. Are you glad when you obey God and do what He says? How would you feel if you didn't?

LEARN

From this story, you learn about OBEDIENCE to God. Abram obeyed God, even when it would have been much easier not to obey.

DO

Did you obey your parents the last time one of them asked you to do something? If you did, you were happy, weren't you? But if you didn't, you were sad. Put a sheet of paper in your room. Each time you obey, draw a small smiling face on the paper. Each time you do not obey, draw a small sad face on the paper. How many happy faces, or sad faces, do you have by bedtime tonight?

17

God Takes Care of Hagar

A Story about PROVIDING

For many years God promised Abraham and Sarah a son. But as they grew older past the time when people have babies, they wondered about God's promise and became more anxious with each passing year. One day Sarah thought she would wait no longer. She urged Abraham to live with her servant girl Hagar so that he could have a baby through her. Sarah would pretend that Hagar's son was hers.

Sarah's foolish plan soon went wrong. When Hagar had a son, and named him Ishmael, Sarah grew jealous and angry, and began to be mean to Hagar.

At last Sarah had a son and named him Isaac. But she grew even more jealous of Hagar now and nagged Abraham to send Hagar and Ishmael away. "Your heir must be my son Isaac, not Ishmael!" Sarah insisted.

Abraham worried and wondered what he should do until God spoke to him. "Do what Sarah wants," God said. "I will make a great nation of each of your sons."

With great sorrow Abraham sent Hagar and Ishmael to live in the hot dry wilderness. Before long, when her water was gone, Hagar sat down and cried, sure that her son would soon die.

But God saw Hagar in her time of trouble and showed her a well of water. Eagerly Hagar filled her water pot and tenderly gave her son Ishmael a drink. His life, and hers, were spared. God had provided!

Through the years, God continued to provide for Hagar and Ishmael as they lived in that place. God kept his promise too, for Ishmael grew to become the head of a great nation.

THINK

1. How did God provide for Hagar and Ishmael in the wilderness? 2. What would have happened if God had not sent His angel to show Hagar a well of water? 3. What does God provide for you each day? Can you name five important things?

LEARN

From this story you learn how God provides. He takes care of us each day, as He did Hagar and Ishmael.

DO

What five things did you list that God provides? Will you thank God now for each one of them?

Abraham Offers Isaac

A Story about TRUST

"Take your son Isaac to the land of Moriah," God told Abraham. "Offer him there as a burnt offering."

Abraham could hardly believe what he heard. "Isaac? A burnt offering? Why?" Why would God tell Abraham to offer his son, the son for whom he and Sarah had waited so many years? Abraham could not think of a reason why. But he trusted God completely. He would do whatever God told him to do.

Surely Abraham loved Isaac as much as any father loved his son. He and Sarah had waited and prayed for this son for such a long time. While they waited and prayed, God kept promising that he would be born. Abraham kept trusting God to keep His promise. At last Isaac was born when Abraham was a hundred years old.

Imagine a hundred-year-old man picking up his first baby! Think of the tears that came to his eyes and the smile that came upon his face.

As Isaac grew up, he and Abraham took care of their sheep together. They fixed their tents together. And they did so many other things that fathers and sons do together.

Now Abraham must give up this son. How could he do it? He did not know. But he would do what God said because he trusted Him to do what was right.

The next morning Abraham headed toward Moriah with Isaac, two young servant boys, and wood for the fire. On the third day, Abraham saw the place where they were going. Leaving the servant boys at the foot of the mountain, Abraham and Isaac went up to the place where the offering was to be made. By this time Isaac began to wonder. "Where is the lamb for the offering?" he asked his father.

"God will provide," Abraham answered. Abraham still trusted God to provide some way to keep him from offering his beloved son. Still waiting for God's other way, Abraham laid the wood on the altar, placed Isaac upon it, and lifted his knife to kill him.

Suddenly God called to Abraham, "Stop! Do not hurt Isaac! I know now that you trust Me completely." Then God showed Abraham a ram caught in some bushes.

"You have trusted Me completely," God said to Abraham. "Because you did, I will bless you and your descendants in wonderful ways." Abraham was glad that he had trusted God.

THINK

1. What did God ask Abraham to do? 2. How did Abraham show that he trusted God completely? 3. What do you do to show God that you trust Him? 4. When you read the Bible, whose book are you reading? Why should you do what it says?

LEARN

From this story you learn how Abraham trusted God completely, even when it seemed impossible to do it.

DO

Look up the following verses in the Bible which tell you about trust: Psalm 52:8; Psalm 56:3,4; Proverbs 3:5,6. Ask how you can trust God more because of what you learn here.

Jacob Steals His Brother's Blessing

A Story about HONESTY

Now that Isaac was old and blind, he decided to give his blessing to his older son Esau. This was very important to a son, for it had to do with leading the family when the father died.

While Esau was his father's favorite son, Jacob was his mother's favorite. She heard about the blessing and made plans for Jacob to get it instead of Esau.

"I heard your father tell Esau to hunt a wild animal and cook it for him," Rebekah told Jacob. "We must cook some goat meat while he is gone. You will take it to your father and he will give you his blessing."

Jacob was afraid, but he did what his mother said. Then he put goat hair on his neck and hands so they would feel more like Esau's hairy skin.

As soon as the meat was cooked, Jacob took it to his father's tent. "My father," Jacob said when he went in. "Who is it?" Isaac asked.

"I am Esau, your firstborn," Jacob lied. "Eat my meat and give me your blessing."

Isaac was suspicious. He thought the voice was Jacob's, but he was too blind to see who it was. So he called Jacob to him and felt his hands and neck.

"The voice is Jacob's, but the hands are Esau's," Isaac said. "Are you really my son Esau?"

Jacob had to lie again. "I am," he said. When he said that, Isaac ate the meat and gave Jacob the blessing, thinking he was Esau. Then he settled down to rest as Jacob quickly left the tent. Jacob had deceived his father and had stolen his brother's blessing.

Jacob had just left when Esau came into the tent with his meat. "Eat my meat and give me your blessing," Esau said to his father.

Isaac sat up, surprised at what he heard. "Who are you?" he asked.

Now Esau was surprised. "I'm your son Esau," he answered.

When Isaac told Esau what had happened, Esau gave a loud, bitter cry. "Bless me too!" he begged.

"Your brother has stolen your blessing," said Isaac. "He is now head of the family and you must serve him."

Esau was so angry that he vowed that he would kill his brother Jacob. Of course Jacob and his mother heard about that and it soon became clear that Jacob must go away from home to live. He had stolen his father's blessing but now he could not live with his family.

THINK

1. What did Jacob do that was not honest? 2. How did this affect his family? 3. Which family members were hurt by Jacob's dishonesty? How?

LEARN

From this story you learn that people often get what they want by being dishonest, but someone usually gets hurt.

DO

Using a sheet of construction paper, make a green tree. Cut out nine pieces of fruit from other colors on construction paper. Now turn to Galatians 5:22 and write one type of "fruit" on each of these. Put them on your tree. Whenever you are tempted to lie or be dishonest, look at the fruit. Ask which fruit you want but feel you will not have because of the lie or dishonesty.

Jacob Marries Rachel

A Story about LOVE

"Where are you from?" Jacob asked the shepherds who sat talking by a well.

"Haran," the shepherds answered. Jacob smiled. At last he had found someone who could show him the way to Haran. He had come hundreds of miles to find his uncle Laban who lived there. Somewhere in Laban's family Jacob hoped to find the girl he would marry.

"Do you know Laban?" Jacob asked.

"Yes, of course we know him," said the shepherds. "Here comes his daughter Rachel with the family sheep."

Jacob watched the young lady with the sheep. So this was Laban's daughter. How beautiful she was. Could this be the girl he would marry? If so, would he love her?

Jacob wanted to be alone with Rachel when he met her. Why did those shepherds have to be there?

"Why don't you water your sheep and get them back to pasture?" Jacob asked the shepherds.

"We don't do things that way," said the shepherds. Besides, they wanted to see what would happen.

By this time, Rachel had come to the well with her sheep. Jacob wasn't sure how to introduce himself, so he ran to the well, rolled the stone from it and began to water her sheep. Then Jacob told Rachel that he was her cousin, the son of her Aunt Rebekah. He was so happy that he kissed Rachel and began to cry.

Jacob fell in love with Rachel. He loved her so much that he worked 14 years for her father so that he could marry her. Don't you think that Rachel must have loved Jacob for doing this?

THINK

1. When you love someone, how much are you willing to do for them? 2. How much did Jacob do to show his love for Rachel? 3. How do you think Rachel felt about Jacob because he worked 14 years to marry her? 4. What special things do you do for those you love most?

LEARN

From this story, you learn that you should do much more than is expected for someone you love.

DO

Cut seven small cards, one for each day this week. Write on each something special you would like to do for your mother, father, brother, sister, or someone else you love. Put the day of the week on the card and give it to this person. Be sure to do that special thing on the day you promise. And be sure not to promise something you will not do.

Joseph Is Sold as a Slave

A Story about JEALOUSY

Everyone knew that Joseph was Jacob's favorite son. Jacob did not try to hide this. Of course this made Joseph's other brothers jealous. They grew even more jealous when Jacob gave Joseph a beautiful robe that was much better than theirs.

One night Joseph dreamed that he and his brothers were binding stalks of grain into sheaves. Joseph's sheaf of grain suddenly stood up and his brothers' sheaves bowed down before it. Joseph told his brothers about this dream and their jealousy turned to hatred. "Do you think you will rule over us some day?" they complained.

This jealous hatred kept troubling the brothers, but they did nothing about it. Then Joseph dreamed another dream. This time the sun, moon and eleven stars bowed down before him. Joseph told this dream to his brothers and his father.

Joseph's father Jacob was disturbed about the dream. "What is this?" he asked. "Will your mother and I and your brothers bow to the ground before you?" Of course the brothers' jealousy grew increasingly worse.

One day Joseph's brothers were taking care of the family sheep many miles north of their home. "Go find them, and make sure that all is well," Jacob told Joseph.

Jacob should never have sent his teenage son to visit the older brothers in a place that far from home. He should have known how jealous they were. But Jacob, like any father, could not think that one brother would hurt another.

When Joseph's brothers saw him coming, they talked angrily with one another. Their jealous hatred had been kept to themselves. Now it was turning the brothers into Joseph's enemies.

"Let's kill him," they said. "We will dump him into a cistern and tell our father a wild animal ate him. That will stop those dreams!"

Reuben, the oldest brother was afraid. He tried to stop the others. "We must not kill him," he said. "Let's just put him into the cistern like a prison instead." Reuben hoped to come back and rescue Joseph.

As soon as Joseph reached the brothers, they grabbed him, tore off his beautiful robe, and threw him into an empty cistern. Then they sat down to eat their lunch.

Before they could eat, the brothers saw a caravan of traders coming. Then Judah had an idea. "Let's sell Joseph to those traders," he said. "Then we will not have to kill him.

The brothers knew that Joseph would suffer much as a slave. He would probably die before long, as many slaves did. But they sold him anyway.

As the caravan disappeared beyond the horizon, the brothers must have wondered what they had done. But it was too late now. They had sold their own brother as a slave. Their jealousy would make them all suffer.

THINK

1. Why were Joseph's brothers jealous? 2. What did Jacob do to make them jealous? What did Joseph do to make them jealous? 3. How did their jealousy make Joseph suffer? 4. How do you think the brothers suffered after Joseph was sold?

LEARN

From this story you learn that jealousy causes people to do terrible things.

DO

Write down the name of someone who has done something, or has something that makes you jealous. Talk with your mother or father to see what you should do about this.

Joseph In Prison

A Story about FAITHFULNESS

When Joseph arrived in Egypt, he was sold as a slave to Potiphar, an officer for pharaoh, the king. He was a kind man and treated Joseph well. Joseph worked faithfully for Potiphar, careful to do more than Potiphar expected him to do.

Potiphar was pleased with Joseph and gave him better work. One day he put him in charge of his entire household. No one was more important then than Joseph, except Potiphar and his family. Potiphar could see that Joseph was faithful to God and that God was with Joseph.

But Potiphar's wife fell in love with Joseph. She wanted Joseph to pretend that he was her husband. Joseph would not do that. He knew that he must be faithful to his master Potiphar. If he did what Potiphar's wife wanted, he could not be trusted.

Potiphar's wife was angry when Joseph turned away from her. She made up a story and told it to her husband, accusing Joseph of doing what she had wanted him to do. Potiphar believed his wife and angrily had Joseph thrown into prison.

Joseph could have blamed God for letting this happen. He could have pouted and sulked, but he didn't. Instead, he was faithful to the warden, the man in charge of the prison, and did even more than he expected. The warden saw that Joseph could be trusted with anything and put him in charge of the other prisoners.

While Joseph was in prison, two of pharaoh's officers were put there also. One night pharaoh's cupbearer, one of the men, dreamed that he squeezed grapes into a cup and gave the cup to pharaoh. The other man, pharaoh's baker, dreamed that birds ate bread from baskets on his head.

"Your dream means that you will go back to work for pharaoh," Joseph told the cupbearer. "Remember me when you do."

"But your dream means that pharaoh will put you to death," Joseph told the baker.

On the third day after that, pharaoh had a birthday party. He gave a feast for his officers and brought his cupbearer back to work. But he had his baker put to death, just as Joseph had said.

The cupbearer forgot about Joseph, his companion in prison. But Joseph, even though he remained in prison, was faithful in all that he did.

LEARN

From the story, you learn that people appreciate a faithful person, even though some may forget about that faithfulness for a short time.

DO

Look up the following Bible verses. They tell about the kind of faithfulness that Joseph had: Psalm 31:23; Proverbs 13:17; Matthew 25:21; 1 Timothy 1:12.

THINK

1. How was Joseph faithful to Potiphar? How did Potiphar reward Joseph for his faithfulness? 2. How was Joseph faithful in prison? How did the warden reward Joseph? 3. How did the cupbearer forget about Joseph and his faithful work? How can you be faithful in your home and school?

Joseph Becomes Governor

A Story about HUMILITY

Days and weeks passed and Joseph was still in prison. He must have wondered if he would ever get out. He had been faithful to God, but that didn't seem to matter, for nothing happened to take him from prison or from being a slave. During all this time, though, Joseph kept humble before God. He never doubted and always seemed to put God first.

One night pharaoh, king of Egypt, had two strange dreams. When he woke up the dreams still disturbed him, so he sent for his magicians. But they could not tell him what the dreams meant.

Then pharaoh's cupbearer remembered Joseph. He told pharaoh how Joseph had known the meaning of his dream about the grapes.

Pharaoh quickly sent for Joseph. He told Joseph about his dreams. In one dream seven lean cows ate seven fat cows. In the other, seven withered heads of grain ate seven good head of grain.

"I hear that you can tell what dreams mean," said pharaoh.

Joseph could have taken all the credit. He could have bragged to pharaoh about how good he was at telling the meaning of dreams. But he didn't. Joseph always gave God the credit for such things. He was truly a humble man.

"I can't tell the meaning of dreams, but God can," said Joseph. "There are seven years of good crops in Egypt now. But after they have ended, there will be seven years of famine. Look for a wise man and put him in charge of the land. Have him collect a fifth of all the harvest and store it for the time of famine."

Pharaoh and his officers liked this plan. "Who is better for the job than you?" pharaoh said to Joseph. "The spirit of God is with you."

That day pharaoh made Joseph governor of Egypt. He gave Joseph the king's official signet ring, the one used to mark in wax on important papers showing they came from the king. He gave Joseph fine clothes, a beautiful wife from an important family, and one of the best chariots in the land.

Joseph came before pharaoh that day a slave and a prisoner. He left as governor of all Egypt.

But Joseph remained humble before God. Even as governor, he did not pretend that he was more important than God. And he asked God to be with him as he built granaries and stored grain that would keep Egypt, and his family, from starving.

THINK

1. What did pharaoh ask Joseph to do for him? Why didn't Joseph say he could tell what dreams meant? 2. How did Joseph show that he was humble? 3. In what ways can you be humble or proud?

LEARN

From this story, you learn that great people are often humble. Sometimes the greatest people are the most humble.

DO

Look up Matthew 23:12. It tells what happened to Joseph, who humbled himself and was exalted as governor of Egypt. Would you like to memorize this verse?

Joseph Forgives His Brothers

A Story about FORGIVENESS

"Where are you from?" the governor of Egypt demanded. The visitors bowed down before him with their faces to the ground. How could they know that this tall powerful man was their brother Joseph, the one they had sold as a slave years before? As they bowed, Joseph remembered his dream as a teenager, when his brothers' sheaves of grain bowed down to his.

"We are from Canaan," the brothers answered. "We have come to buy food."

"You are spies," Joseph shouted. "You want to find where our land is weak." Joseph was about to put his brothers through some hard tests. He must have wanted to reach out to them, to tell them who he was. But he must first learn if they were sorry for what they had done.

"We are twelve brothers," they said "Our youngest brother is home with our father. The other is dead."

"I will find out if you are telling the truth," said Joseph. "You must bring your younger brother here. If you don't, I will know that you are lying." Joseph had his brothers put into prison. They must learn what it was like to live in a dark, foul prison in Egypt.

After three days, Joseph took the brothers out again. "One of you must stay here in prison until the others return with your younger brother," he said. "Take grain back home to your hungry families, but your brother will not be set free until you return."

"We are being punished for what we did to Joseph," the brothers said to one another. They did not know that Joseph understood what they said, for he had been speaking through a man who knew both languages.

"I told you not to hurt Joseph," said Reuben. "But you wouldn't listen to me."

When Joseph heard what the brothers said, he turned away from them and wept. Now he had heard for the first time that they were truly sorry that they had sold him as a slave.

Joseph ordered Simeon to be bound while the other brothers watched. Then he quietly gave orders for his brothers' sacks to be filled with grain and their money put into their sacks. Of course, when the brothers opened their sacks later and found the money, they were afraid. "What is God doing to us?" they asked.

Jacob was disturbed when he heard what had happened to Simeon. He was even more disturbed to hear that the governor had demanded that Benjamin come to Egypt. If he did not, the brothers could not buy grain and Simeon would not go free.

Jacob refused to let Benjamin go, even though Reuben promised to be personally responsible and take special care of him.

Then the famine grew worse. The corn they had brought from Egypt was all gone and Jacob had to send his sons back to Egypt to buy more. But they were afraid and would not go unless Benjamin went with them. Now Judah also promised to guard him very carefully.

Finally Jacob agreed to let Benjamin go. He also sent a special gift to the governor, along with some fruit, honey, spices and nuts. He told the brothers to take twice as much money with them, and to return the money they had found in their sacks before.

When the brothers arrived in Egypt with Benjamin, Joseph ordered them to come to his house for dinner. They were even more afraid then, and they wondered what the governor would do to them. They thought he would accuse them of stealing the money and that he would make them prisoners.

On the way to Joseph's house, the brothers talked with the man in charge of Joseph's things. "We brought more money because we found our money in the sacks last time," they said.

"Don't worry about it," the man answered. "You paid for the grain. You owe us nothing."

Then he released Simeon from prison and brought him to his brothers.

When Joseph arrived at his house, the brothers were waiting with the gifts they had brought from Canaan. They bowed and he asked about their father. They bowed again and said he was well.

At dinner, Joseph seated the brothers by age. Think how surprised they were when they saw that! But they ate the good food and actually seemed to enjoy this unusual meal.

After dinner the sacks were filled and the men headed home. Of course they did not know that Joseph had had his silver cup hidden in Benjamin's sack. Joseph sent his steward to catch up with the men and when he found the silver cup, the brothers were sure they would all go to prison.

They were terrified as they stood before Joseph and his guard with the silver cup. Joseph told them the one in whose sack the cup had been found would have to be his servant. The rest of them could go home. He wanted to see if they were still jealous or if they really cared about what happened to Benjamin.

Judah quickly begged the governor to let him stay as the servant in Benjamin's place and to let his youngest brother go back to their father.

When he heard that, Joseph could keep

his secret no longer. He sent all the servants out of the room and when he was alone with his brothers, he cried out, "I am Joseph!" Then he began to weep. The brothers were so shocked and afraid they didn't know what to say.

Almost anyone in Joseph's place would have had those brothers punished for selling him as a slave. But not Joseph. "God sent me here to Egypt to save your lives," Joseph told them. Then he forgave them for the things they had done.

This beautiful story of forgiveness ends with Jacob and his entire family moving to Egypt. There Joseph cared for them as long as they lived. So everyone did live happily ever after, because the son who was sold as a slave forgave.

THINK

1. What had Joseph's brothers done to him that was wrong? 2. How could Joseph have gotten even with them when they came to buy grain? Why didn't he? 3. How did he forgive them? How did the story end happily?

LEARN

From this story, you learn that stories and lives end happily when people truly forgive.

DO

Do you need to forgive someone for something that person has done to you? Forgiveness is only one letter or phone call away. Will you write the letter or make that phone call now...and forgive?

God Takes Care of Baby Moses

A Story about PROVIDING

Many years had passed since Joseph's family had moved to Egypt. As the years went by, Joseph and his brothers died, and so did their children and their children's children. New pharaohs came and went too. For a while, the pharaohs remembered how Joseph had saved Egypt from famine and they treated his family well. But at last there came a pharaoh who did not care. He was afraid of these Hebrews, the people descended from Joseph and his brothers, because there were so many of them. "What if they side with our enemies and fight against us?" he wondered.

So this pharaoh put slave masters over the Hebrews and they forced the Hebrews to build cities for the Egyptians. Even so, the Hebrews grew in numbers faster than the Egyptians.

Pharaoh tried to force the Egyptian midwives, women who helped other women have babies, to kill the Hebrew boys as soon as they were born. But the midwives feared God and refused to do it.

At last pharaoh gave orders for every Hebrew baby boy to be thrown into the Nile River. Then he sent his soldiers to see that it was done.

Amram and Jochebed, a Hebrew slave couple, were afraid, for they had just had a new baby boy. If he were found, pharaoh's soldiers would throw him into the river. What could they do to protect him? For three months they tried one way and then another. At last they knew they would soon be discovered.

Then Jochebed had a plan. She wove a basket from the papyrus reeds that grew along the Nile River. She coated it with tar and pitch and hid the basket among the reeds in the shallow part of the river. Miriam, the baby's older sister, sat nearby to watch. Now they must have prayed that God would protect their baby.

One day pharaoh's daughter came to the river to bathe. As she and her attendants walked along the river they heard a baby crying. Pharaoh's daughter looked in the basket and saw the baby. She felt sorry for him and wanted to keep him. She would protect him from pharaoh's soldiers.

Miriam quickly appeared. "Shall I find a Hebrew nurse for you?" she asked.

"Yes," said pharaoh's daughter. Of course Miriam brought her mother.

Pharaoh's daughter named the baby Moses and left him in his mother's care. God had protected Moses in a special way. Moses would be safe now, safe to grow up to serve God, who had taken care of him.

THINK

1. What did Jochebed do to protect Moses? 2. What did Miriam do? 3. How did pharaoh's daughter protect Moses? 4. What do you think God did in all this to protect Moses? 5. Think of some ways God protects you. What are they?

LEARN

From this story, you learn that God protects in wonderful ways.

DO

On a sheet of paper, or a card, write down five things you think could hurt you. Now pray that God will protect you from them.

Moses at the Burning Bush

A Story about OBEDIENCE

Moses often thought of that day in Egypt when he had killed an Egyptian guard. But what else could he have done? The guard was torturing a Hebrew slave and Moses could not let that happen.

Yet because of that, Moses had to run away from Egypt and hide in Midian. Now he was a shepherd, taking care of his father-in-law's sheep in the wilderness near Mount Sinai.

While Moses was watching the sheep one day, he was startled to see a bush burning, but not burning up. He moved closer and closer to see what was happening. Suddenly a voice called from the bush, "Moses! Moses!"

Moses was afraid. "Here I am," he answered.

"Take off your sandals," the voice called. "The place where you stand is holy ground. I am the God of your father, the God of Abraham, Isaac, and Jacob."

When Moses heard that, he hid his face. He was afraid to look at God, for it was said that to look at God would cause death.

"I have seen the suffering of my people in Egypt," God said. "I will rescue them. You must go back to Egypt to lead them out of their slavery."

Moses was afraid to go back to Egypt, so he began to make excuses, but it was no use. God had chosen him to lead his people from Egypt. Moses must go. He knew he would suffer and face much trouble. But when God says go, why should anyone say no? So Moses obeyed God and went back to Egypt. Wouldn't you?

THINK

1. Why did Moses not want to go back to Egypt? 2. What did God want him to do there? 3. Why did Moses obey God? 4. Why should you obey God?

LEARN

From this story, you learn that you should obey God.

DO

Draw a big O on a piece of paper. Now put a B lying across the inside to form eyes, add an E lying across where the mouth should go and add a small Y for the nose. You have a little face to put on your wall to remind you to OBEY.

The Ten Plagues

A Story about POWER

Who is more powerful, the God of Moses and his people or the gods of the Egyptians? Pharaoh thought his gods were more powerful. But Moses knew that God was greater.

For many years, pharaoh had kept Moses' people, the Hebrews, in slavery. He had made them work hard, building cities for him. Of course pharaoh did not pay them. He gave them only enough food to keep them strong for his work, and a tiny hut to live in.

God did not want His people to be slaves. Moses did not want his people to be slaves either. But as long as pharaoh thought his gods were greater than Moses' god, he would not let these people go free.

That is why God spoke to Moses in a special way and sent him back to Egypt. God wanted Moses to tell pharaoh to let the people go. And God chose Moses' brother Aaron to help him.

"God says you must let my people go free," Moses told pharaoh. But pharaoh was angry. He would not give up all that free work.

"Who is your God, and why should I do what He says?" pharaoh asked. "Show me how powerful He is."

Aaron threw down his shepherd's rod and it became a snake. Surely no one else could do that. But pharaoh's magicians had some strange power. When they threw down their rods, they became snakes too. You can imagine how surprised Moses and Aaron were to see that! But God showed He was more powerful than the Egyptian gods. Aaron's snake ate up all the other snakes! It didn't convince pharaoh, though. He still thought his gods were as powerful as the God of Moses and his people.

On the next visit, Moses and Aaron caused the first of the ten plagues to come to the land of Egypt. Each of them became more terrible than the one before. The first was the plague of blood, when Moses touched the Nile River and the water turned to blood. Somehow, pharaoh's magicians could do this too. So pharaoh still didn't think the God of Moses was more powerful than the gods of Egypt.

Moses and Aaron came back to pharaoh to bring another plague. This time they caused frogs to come up on the land by the thousands. But pharaoh's magicians could do this too. So pharaoh still thought his gods were as powerful as the God of Moses and his people.

The next time Moses and Aaron came to pharaoh, they caused a plague of lice or gnats to go on all the animals of Egypt. Pharaoh's magicians could not do this. Now the magicians began to see how much power God had. But pharaoh's heart was hard and he wouldn't listen to them.

Swarms of flies came next. This time Moses told pharaoh that God would divide the people and the flies would only come upon the Egyptians. God would not let them come to His people. After God sent the flies, pharaoh said the people should worship their God but they could not go free.

The next plague God sent caused the cattle, the horses, and many other animals to become sick and die. Now pharaoh and his people began to be afraid, for they worshiped the cow and bull. God was showing that He was stronger than the cow god, Hathor, or the bull god, Apis.

Another plague made painful boils break out upon all the Egyptian people and on the animals that were left. Many of the Egyptian people began to believe that the God of Moses was the most powerful. But pharaoh's heart just got harder, and he would not admit it. He still would not let the people go.

When hail came and destroyed most of the crops of Egypt, that showed that God was greater than all the Egyptian gods of the harvest. Now pharaoh sent for Moses and Aaron. He told them he was wrong. If they would stop the hail, he would let the people go. When Moses and Aaron stopped the hail, though, pharaoh changed his mind. He would not let the people of Israel go free.

When locusts came and destroyed the rest of the crops of Egypt, he did the same thing again.

One day darkness came across the land. It was so thick they could feel it and their lamps wouldn't make any light. But it came only to the Egyptians. God's people, the children of Israel, had light in their homes. The Egyptians thought their greatest god of all, Re, the god of the sun, had died in his nightly journey under the earth. They thought he fought a great snake each night and if the snake ever won, the sun would not shine again. So when the sun did not shine for three days, they were sure their greatest god had lost.

Then a plague worse than darkness came. All the firstborn animals and people died, even pharaoh's oldest son. It was clear now that God controlled life and death. Now pharaoh and his people feared Moses' God, for they thought much about life and death, and feared for their own lives.

At last the contest was over. Moses' God was more powerful than all the gods of Egypt. The magicians, the Egyptian people, and even pharaoh, all knew that now.

THINK

1. How do you know that God is more powerful than all the gods of Egypt? 2. Why do you think He is more powerful than anyone else today?

LEARN

From this story, you learn that God is more powerful than anyone else, even the gods of Egypt.

DO

Draw a picture of the three most powerful things you can think of. Think of such things as the sun, a volcano, and storm clouds. Which of these does God control?

The Exodus from Egypt

A Story about OBEDIENCE

"Tell your people to do exactly what I say," the Lord said to Moses. Moses listened carefully. The people listened carefully too when Moses told them what the Lord said.

The Lord told the people how to prepare a special meal, called the Passover. He told them what meat to use, how to eat it, and how to sprinkle the lamb's blood on the doorposts of their homes.

"I will pass through Egypt and will strike every firstborn man and animal," the Lord warned. "When I see the blood on a doorpost, I will pass over you."

The Hebrews did exactly what the Lord said. But of course the Egyptians did not. That night the angel of death passed through Egypt. All firstborn men and animals died, except in houses with the blood on the doorposts.

The people of Egypt were terrified. There was hardly a home in Egypt where the angel of death had not touched some relative. Now the Egyptians were pleading for the Hebrews to leave. They were so anxious that they gave jewelry and gold and precious gifts to get them on their way.

At last pharaoh called for Moses and Aaron. "Go! Get out of the land!" he urged.

The people of Israel, the Hebrews, were free! What a procession they made as they left the city and went their way through the wilderness toward the Promised Land. They were safe and they were free because they had obeyed the Lord completely.

THINK

1. What do you think would have happened if the people had not obeyed the Lord completely? 2. What happened to the Hebrews, the people of Israel, because they did obey? 3. Why should you obey the Lord? 4. Why should you obey your parents?

LEARN

From this story, you learn that good things happen to those who obey the Lord.

DO

Tell this story again, but pretend that Moses' people refused to obey the Lord. How would the story go on from there?

Crossing the Red Sea

A Story about TRUST

"What have we done?" pharaoh began to wonder. "We have let all those slaves go free and have lost their work."

Pharaoh had begun to see how much work the Hebrews had done. Now that they were gone, who was there to do this work? He began to see how much work would not get done without them.

Pharaoh ordered men to get his chariot and prepare his army for battle. He had heard how the Hebrews were moving about in the wilderness and thought they must surely not know where they were going. His spies must have told him how the Israelites were trapped at a camp by the sea and how easy it would be to conquer them there.

So pharaoh's chariots, horsemen, and troops pursued as quickly as they could and found the Israelites trapped by the sea. Moses knew why they were there, of course, for the Lord had told him. But the people of Israel did not know. They were terrified to see pharaoh and his chariots and horsemen approaching. They were sure that they could not escape for they did not trust the Lord to save them. Some began to complain to Moses.

"Why have you brought us out here to die?" they said. "Didn't we tell you to leave us in Egypt? It would be better to serve the Egyptians there than die out here."

"Don't be afraid," said Moses. "Trust the Lord and see how He will deliver you. The Lord will fight for you."

As evening came, the Lord moved the cloud that led the Israelites until it was between them and the Egyptians. The Egyptian army had to stop, for they could not see where they were going.

At the Lord's command, Moses stretched out his rod and his hand across the sea. All night the Lord drove the sea apart with a strong wind and made a path across the sea on dry land. When morning came, Moses led his people to the other side of the sea, with a wall of water on each side of them. Moses and his people trusted God to keep the water there until they had crossed.

At the right moment, the Lord took His cloud away, and the Egyptian army pursued. But when they reached the sea, the Lord let the waters rush back upon them and they were drowned.

Now the people of Israel saw how the Lord could do great miracles to save His people. They knew that they had not trusted Him

fully. It was an important lesson for them to learn, one they would have to learn again and again in the wilderness.

THINK

1. Why did pharaoh go after the people of Israel? 2. How did the people of Israel fail to trust the Lord to take care of them? 3. How did they learn that they could trust the Lord and He would take care of them? 4. What did you learn about trusting the Lord?

LEARN

From this story, you learn that you can trust the Lord and He will take care of you.

DO

Psalm 56:3,4 are good verses to memorize. So are Proverbs 3:5,6. Would you like to memorize one pair of these now?

Israel in the Wilderness

A Story about PROVIDING

There were no grocery stores in the wilderness, no wells, no gardens or vineyards, and no rivers where the people could fish. The people had never lived in the wilderness before, so they began to worry about food and water. All that first day in the wilderness they marched over the hot sands but found no food or water. The second day was just like the first. By this time the people were getting frantic. Then the third day came. Still no food or water. The situation looked desperate! At last they came to a spring. They could hardly wait to drink. Imagine how disappointed they were to find that the water was bitter.

Moses cried to the Lord and the Lord showed him some wood. When he put it into the water, it became sweet and the people could drink it.

Step by step through the wilderness it was this way. At one place, the Lord led the people to some springs with palm trees around them. At another place he showed Moses how to strike a rock to get water. But always there was enough water, for the Lord provided.

There was also the problem of food. The Lord provided that, too. Each day He sent little flakes of food called manna. There was always enough. The Israelites did not starve in the wilderness, for the Lord was with them. He always provided enough for each day.

THINK

1. Did any of the Israelites starve to death or die of thirst in the wilderness? 2. Who took care of them and provided food and water? 3. Has the Lord provided enough food and water for you each day?

LEARN

From this story, you learn that God does provide, giving you enough food and water for each day.

DO

Draw some of the different places where God provides water for you. Don't forget a faucet, a drinking fountain, a pump, and a stream. Can you think of others?

The Ten Commandments

A Story about OBEDIENCE

Most people don't like to obey orders. They like to do what they want to do, not what someone else tells them. But the Lord knew that people could not live that way. Things would get too confusing.

When the people of Israel reached Mount Sinai, the Lord told Moses to set up camp. He and the Israelites would stay there for quite some time. They would build a tent where they could worship the Lord, and He would give them His laws through Moses.

The Lord gave Moses many laws for the people to follow. But ten of them seemed more important than the others. Perhaps that is because the Lord thought they were so important that He wrote them Himself, with His own finger, on tablets of stone. Then He gave them to Moses on the top of Mount Sinai.

Today people still try to follow these ten laws, called The Ten Commandments. Do you know them? This is what they say: 1. Do not worship any other gods instead of Me. 2. Do not make idols or worship them. 3. Do not use the Lord's name in the wrong way. 4. Honor the Lord on the seventh day. 5. Honor your father and mother. 6. Do not murder. 7. Do not pretend someone else's husband or wife is yours. 8. Do not steal. 9. Do not lie. 10. Do not want what belongs to someone else.

These are all good laws, aren't they? They are even good enough for us to remember and obey today.

THINK

1. How important are The Ten Commandments? 2. Do you try to do what they say? 3. Jesus said that following The Ten Commandments is not enough to get us to heaven. We must accept Him to do that. But they are important for us to follow, so that we can please Him.

LEARN

From this story, you learn that God's rules are good rules and help us please Him.

DO

Have you ever memorized The Ten Commandments? It's hard to do if you learn the entire Bible section. But you can memorize the short statements in this story. Would you like to do that?

Twelve Spies Visit Canaan

A Story about TRUST

"Send some men to explore the land," the Lord told Moses. The land was The Promised Land, which the Lord promised to give to Moses and his people. But they would have to go in and take it.

Moses chose one man from each of the twelve tribes. Then he sent them into The Promised Land to explore.

"What kind of land is it? Is it good or bad? What kind of towns do the people live in? Do the towns have walls and forts? Is the soil good or poor? Are there trees? What kinds of fruits grow there?" These were questions the spies were to answer.

So the twelve spies went into The Promised Land. They went through the land, from one end to the other. On their way back, they stopped in the Valley of Eshcol and cut a large bunch of grapes. It was so large that two men had to carry it on a pole. They also carried pomegranates and figs.

When the spies returned, they gave their report to Moses and the leaders. "The land is rich, but the people are powerful," they said. "They live in large cities with walls and forts. Some of the people are giants."

One of the twelve spies, Caleb, asked the people to be quiet while he spoke. "We should go into this land and take possession," said Caleb. "We can do it!" Caleb trusted the Lord to help them win.

But ten of the spies did not trust the Lord to help them win.

"The men are too powerful," they argued. "We looked like grasshoppers beside them."

That night the people of Israel grumbled against Moses and Aaron. They talked about getting new leaders and going back to Egypt. Then Moses and Aaron fell on their faces before the Lord in front of all the people, begging the Lord for His help.

Joshua, one of the spies, urged the people to go into the land and take it. "Don't rebel against the Lord," he said. "The Lord is with us." Like Caleb, Joshua showed that he trusted the Lord to help them.

But the people refused to listen. They even talked about stoning Moses and Aaron. Then the Lord appeared at the tabernacle and spoke. "Not one person who rebelled against Me and failed to trust Me will go into The Promised Land," He said. "Every grownup will die in the wilderness except Joshua and Caleb. Then, when your children grow up, they will be able to go into The Promised Land." When the people heard that, they were sorry that they had not trusted the Lord, but it was too late now.

THINK

1. What great miracles had the Lord done for these people since they left Egypt? Why should those miracles have shown them that they could trust the Lord for help? 2. Why should you trust the Lord to help you each day?

LEARN

From this story, you learn that the Lord will do great and wonderful things if we trust Him.

DO

Do you remember the bunch of grapes the people brought back? Draw a bunch of grapes like that on some paper. Put one of these letters in each grape: T R U S T. What should that help you remember to do?

Rahab Helps Two Spies

A Story about KINDNESS

"Go into The Promised Land and find out what you can," Joshua told two spies. "Look especially at Jericho."

The people of Israel were ready to go into The Promised Land to live. But they must first fight the people who lived there, and conquer them. If they didn't, they would be driven back into the wilderness or would all be killed.

The two spies crossed the Jordan River and went to Jericho. That was the first city the Israelites must conquer. The spies must learn whatever they could to help their people win in a battle.

The spies stayed at a house built on Jericho's wall. The owner, a woman named Rahab, rented rooms to travelers. But someone saw the men come into Jericho and told the king. The king sent men to capture them.

When Rahab heard that the king's men were coming, she hid the spies under some flax on her rooftop. Then she told the king's men, "They were here, but they left just before sunset in time to get outside the city gate. Hurry, and you may catch them."

As soon as the king's men left, Rahab went up to the rooftop to have a talk with the spies. "I know that the Lord has already given this land to you," she said. "Our people are afraid of you because of the miracles which the Lord has done for you. I have shown kindness to you by keeping you safe, so please show kindness to me and my family when you conquer Jericho."

"You have been kind and saved our lives, so we will be kind and save yours," the spies said. "But you must tie this scarlet cord in your window. When we come to conquer, whoever is in the house will be saved. Whoever is outside the house will be killed."

Rahab agreed, and tied the scarlet cord in her window. It would remind the men and their army of Rahab's kindness, and of their promise to be kind to her.

THINK

1. How was Rahab kind to the two spies? Why did she do this? 2. How did Rahab want the spies and their army to be kind to her? 3. How would the Israelite army know Rahab's house? 4. How has the Lord been kind to you? 5. What can you do to say thank you and show kindness in return?

LEARN

From this story, you learn that one kindness deserves another. When someone is kind to you, be kind to that person also.

DO

Ask your mother to help you find a red string, piece of yarn, or thread, and hang it in your window this week. Each time you see it, remember to be kind to others, especially to your family.

57

Crossing the Jordan River

A Story about DEDICATION

For the last 40 years the people of Israel had traveled through the wilderness, headed for The Promised Land. They dreamed of the day when they would get there, settle down, build their homes, and plant their gardens and vineyards. Most of the people who started on this long trip had died in the wilderness, but their children had grown up and had come at last to the Jordan River. As soon as they crossed the river, they would be in the land that the Lord had promised them.

On the night before they crossed the river, Joshua spoke to the people. "Dedicate yourselves to the Lord," Joshua told the people. "Tomorrow the Lord will do amazing things for you."

The people dedicated themselves to the Lord. They promised to do exactly what He said.

The next day, Joshua told the people how the Lord wanted them to cross the river. Because the people had dedicated themselves to the Lord, they did exactly what the Lord told them through Joshua.

"Carry the ark of the covenant into the river," Joshua told the priests. They did exactly what Joshua said. When they stepped into the river, the water stopped so the priests walked out to the middle of the riverbed on dry ground. Then the people crossed to the other side without getting their feet wet.

"Come up out of the riverbed, to the other side," Joshua told the priest who carried the ark. When they did exactly what Joshua said, the water filled the river again. The people were all safe now in The Promised Land.

"Put twelve stones into a pile," Joshua ordered. "They will help you remember what the Lord has done today." They did exactly what the Lord said through Joshua. They were glad, too, for the stones reminded them often how the Lord had helped them go into the land He had promised.

THINK

1. When the people dedicated themselves to the Lord, what did they promise to do? 2. How did they keep their promise? 3. What did they do to remind them of all that the Lord had done that day?

LEARN

From this story, you learn that when you dedicate yourself to the Lord, you do exactly what He wants. This is good to remember, isn't it?

DO

It is good to have something nearby to remind us of the Lord. Your Bible lying in your room reminds you to read it. A motto, or Bible verse, on your wall reminds you to pray or please the Lord some other way. Some people put pictures of missionaries on their wall to remember to pray for them. Put up something today to remind you to do something the Lord wants you to do.

Joshua Captures Jericho

A Story about OBEDIENCE

"Obey Me and Jericho will be yours," the Lord said to Joshua. Joshua listened carefully. He remembered what had happened before. Whenever the people of Israel obeyed the Lord, He helped them. When they did not obey Him, they got into trouble.

Joshua called his people together. Then he told them what the Lord had said. "Obey the Lord and He will help us capture the city," Joshua said.

Joshua's soldiers should have been afraid. Jericho had great walls and mighty warriors. How could they hope to get into the city to fight? How could they get over those walls?

But Joshua's soldiers were not afraid. Instead, the people of Jericho were afraid. They had heard how the Lord had helped the people of Israel on the way to The Promised Land.

"March around Jericho six days," Joshua commanded. Seven priests went first, blowing their trumpets, followed by more priests who carried the ark of the covenant. An armed guard went before the trumpeters, and another armed guard followed the ark. Israel's fighting men followed.

Each day for six days the Israelites marched around Jericho once. On the seventh day they marched around the city seven times. Then Joshua commanded, "Shout, for the Lord has given you the city."

The people shouted and Jericho's walls came tumbling down. The people of Israel had done exactly what the Lord said. The city of Jericho was theirs.

THINK

1. What did the Lord tell the Israelites to do to conquer Jericho? 2. What did the Israelites do? 3. What might have been different if they had not obeyed the Lord completely?

LEARN

From this story, you learn that it is important to obey the Lord.

DO

Who should you obey? What about your parents? What about the Lord? Draw a smiling face on a card. That will help you remember to obey your parents. Draw a rectangle and write Bible on it. That will help you remember to obey the Lord, and to do what He says in His Word. Keep these in a place where you will see them often.

Gideon's 300

A Story about COURAGE

"You have too many soldiers," the Lord told Gideon. Gideon was surprised. How can an army have too many soldiers, especially when it is going to fight a much larger army?

Gideon was going out to fight the Midianites, a tribe of people who had been stealing the Israelite crops and leaving the people hungry. Once and for all he and his men must defeat these enemies or the Israelites would starve.

"If you win the battle with that many men, you will think your army did it without My help and will brag about it," the Lord said. "Send home the men who are afraid."

When Gideon told his army what the Lord said, 22,000 men went home. They did not have the courage to fight. There were only 10,000 left. "There are still too many," the Lord said. Then the Lord told Gideon how to keep only the very best. Gideon did exactly what the Lord said. He led his men down to a stream and told them to drink. Those who bent down and lapped the water like animals were sent home. They were not careful soldiers, for they could not see while they were drinking. Those who scooped water into their hands and looked around while they drank were kept. But there were only 300 of them. Those men had to have the courage to stay and fight with Gideon.

Gideon and his 300 listened carefully to the Lord. He told them what to do. In the middle of the night, they went up to a hill surrounding the enemy camp with trumpets, torches, and clay pitchers. They covered their torches with the pitchers and at a signal from Gideon, broke the pitchers, blew on the trumpets, and shouted. The enemy soldiers were completely surprised and thought they were outnumbered, so they began to fight each other. Each thought the others were Gideon's soldiers.

The 300 soldiers of Gideon could never brag that they had won the battle. The Lord had told them what to do. He had been with them and had helped them defeat a great army.

How did these men have so much courage? Because they trusted the Lord, they could do things the way He said. That's a good rule for us to remember, too.

THINK

1. Why did the Lord say Gideon had too many soldiers? 2. How did the Lord help Gideon send 32,000 men home? 3. Why do you think Gideon and his 300 men had courage?

LEARN

From this story you learn that you have courage to do what you should when you trust the Lord to help you.

DO

Are you afraid of something or someone? Who can help you? Why not ask Him to help you now?

Samson Marries a Philistine

A Story about SELF-CONTROL

"I want to marry this girl," Samson insisted. Samson's parents could not believe that Samson wanted to marry a Philistine. At this time the Philistines ruled Israel, and the two nations were bitter enemies.

But Samson would not listen to his parents. "Can't you find a wife among our own people?" Samson's parents asked. But Samson would not listen to them. He would do what he wanted to do.

So Samson set out for the Philistine town of Timnah with his mother and father. While his parents were making wedding arrangements, Samson walked alone in a vineyard. Suddenly a fierce young lion leaped at him from the bushes. Samson easily wrestled the lion to the ground and killed it, for the Lord had made Samson the strongest man in Israel.

Soon it was Samson's wedding day and he returned to Timnah. On the way he stopped to look at the young lion he had killed. A swarm of bees had made a nest in the body of the lion and Samson ate some honey.

Samson arrived at the wedding feast and made a deal with the Philistine men there. "If you can guess my riddle in seven days," he said, "I will give each of you two coats. But if you do not guess the riddle, you must each give me two coats." The men agreed and Samson told them this riddle about the lion: "From the eater came something to eat. From the strong came something sweet."

The Philistine men could not guess the riddle. So they went to Samson's wife and said they would kill her if she did not get the answer for them. She nagged Samson so much that finally on the last day, Samson could not control himself and told her the answer. The men then came to Samson and said, "What is sweeter than honey, or stronger than a lion?"

Samson was angry that he had not controlled his tongue and kept the answer a secret. He marched in a rage to the city of Ashkelon, killed thirty Philistine men there, and took their coats to the men at the wedding feast. Then he went home to his parents and left his wife behind.

Samson certainly knew that he had disappointed the Lord. Instead of putting his thoughts and actions under the Lord's control, he did what he wanted.

THINK

1. Who did Samson want to please, the Lord, or himself? 2. How did Samson fail to control his mind and body? 3. Why does the Lord want you to keep control of yourself? How does that please Him?

LEARN

From this story, you learn that you please the Lord by keeping control of yourself.

DO

Memorize Galatians 5:22. The next time you think you are not pleasing the Lord, say the verse to yourself. What should that help you do?

Samson and Delilah

A Story about FAITHFULNESS

Would you like to be the strongest person in the world? Samson was. Because he was so strong, all Israel hoped that Samson would lead them. That is what the Lord wanted too. But Samson was not a good leader because he did not use his strength to please the Lord.

One time Samson spent the night with a Philistine woman in Gaza. Samson knew this was wrong and would not please the Lord. But he did it anyway. The men of Gaza planned to kill him at dawn. They were afraid that Samson might hurt them. So the Philistines surrounded the city and locked the heavy city gate.

But Samson learned of the plot. He got up in the middle of the night, grabbed the wooden doors of the gate, and tore the entire gate from the ground. Then he carried it to the top of a hill far away.

Some time later, Samson fell in love with a Philistine woman named Delilah. When the Philistine rulers found out they told Delilah, "If you can find the secret to Samson's strength, we will make you rich."

One day Delilah said to Samson, "Tell me the secret of your great strength. Can anything take it away?"

"If anyone ties me with seven fresh bowstrings, I will be as weak as any other man," Samson lied. That night when Samson fell asleep, Delilah tied Samson's arms and legs with seven fresh bowstrings. Philistine soldiers were hiding in the other room. "Samson, get up! The Philistines are after you," she shouted. Samson jumped up and snapped the bowstrings as if they were not there.

Again and again Delilah tried to learn the secret of Samson's strength. And each time Samson tricked her by making up a story about the source of his strength. But Delilah nagged him so much that at last he gave in. He foolishly told her the truth. "Long ago I made a vow to God that I would not cut my hair. If I do, I will become as weak as any other man."

That night Samson again fell asleep on Delilah's lap, and she shaved the hair from his head. "Samson, the Philistines are after you!" she shouted. Samson jumped up, but this time his strength was gone. He had broken his promise to God. The Philistines seized him and gouged out his eyes. Then they led him away in chains to prison.

The Lord gave Samson the ability to become a great man. But Samson wasted his time and ability on the wrong people. Samson learned the hard way that it is better to use your strength for the Lord than for yourself.

THINK

1. Who was the strongest man in the world? 2. Who gave him this strength? 3. Did Samson use his strength to please the Lord or to please himself? 4. How should you use your strength?

LEARN

From this story, you learn that you should use your strength to please the Lord.

DO

What do you do best? Do you play an instrument best? Do you play ball best? Or do you do you best in school work? The next time you do what you do best, tell the Lord you are doing it for Him.

67

The Story of Ruth

A Story about LOVE

The rain did not fall and the crops did not grow in Israel for a long time. Some people had to move away because there was no food. One family, Elimelech, Naomi, and their two sons, moved to Moab where the sons married Moabite girls, Ruth and Orpah. As time passed, Elimelech and his two sons died, leaving Naomi alone with these two girls.

One day Naomi decided to return to Israel where many of her people still worshiped God. The people in Moab did not do that. Orpah decided to stay in Moab with her friends, but Ruth went with Naomi. Together the two walked many miles to Bethlehem where Naomi once lived.

Ruth loved Naomi and tried to make her happy. Each day during harvest time Ruth went to the fields which a man named Boaz owned. There she followed the men who cut the stalks of grain and tied them into bundles. She picked up stalks of grain they had left behind and beat the grain from it.

"Who is that young woman?" Boaz asked his men one day. "That is Ruth," the men said. "She is the one who came from Moab with Naomi." Boaz wanted to talk with Ruth. "I have heard that you have been good to your mother-in-law Naomi," Boaz told her. "God will bless you for that." Then Boaz asked Ruth to come to his field each day to pick up grain. "I will take care of you," he said.

Ruth worked faithfully in the fields, and each day brought grain home to Naomi. Boaz began to love Ruth and soon asked her to marry him. Together, Ruth and Boaz took care of Naomi.

God blessed Ruth because she was kind to Naomi, and because she had chosen God as her God. And God was happy that Ruth, Boaz and Naomi loved each other.

THINK

1. How do you know that Ruth loved Naomi? What did Ruth do for her? 2. Who fell in love with Ruth? What did Boaz and Ruth do for Naomi? Why do you think they did this? 3. When you love someone, what will you do for them?

LEARN

From this story, you learn that you do good things for those you love.

DO

How much do you love your parents? Would you like to do something good for them? Write something you would like to do on a card. For example: GOOD FOR WASHING DISHES TONIGHT. Then give it to the parent whom it will help most. Be sure to do what you say.

Samuel—a Boy Who Honored God

A Story about REVERENCE

Someone called Samuel's name! Samuel sat up in bed and looked around his big tent home. He saw nothing but shadows from the flickering yellow light of the oil lamps. The shadows danced upon the golden chest across the room. They played upon the angel-like figures that stood with outstretched wings upon this chest.

The big tent where Samuel lived was God's house. Many years ago Moses and his people had made it in the wilderness. They had carried it here to Shiloh when they came into the Promised Land. Now the boy Samuel lived here and helped the old priest Eli take care of God's house. Eli was glad, for Samuel showed reverence, or honor, for God and Eli's sons did not. So Samuel slept in one of the most important places in God's house, near the golden chest, the Ark of the Covenant. Here he heard God call his name.

"Samuel! Samuel!" God's voice called. Samuel thought Eli was calling. He jumped from his bed and ran to ask Eli what he wanted.

"I did not call you," Eli told Samuel. "Go back to bed."

Samuel went back to bed but soon he heard God's voice calling his name. Again Samuel ran to ask Eli what he wanted.

"I did not call you!" Eli told Samuel. "Go back to bed!"

Once more Samuel heard God's voice calling. Once more he ran to ask Eli what he wanted.

Now Eli knew that God was calling Samuel. He told Samuel that God must have something important to tell him.

"Go back to bed," Eli told Samuel. "When you hear God's voice again, tell Him that you are listening."

When God spoke this time, Samuel listened carefully. "Eli's sons do not honor Me or reverence Me," God told Samuel. "I have warned Eli and his sons, but Eli does nothing to stop them. Now I will punish them."

When morning came, Eli made Samuel tell him what God said. Of course Eli was sad. But he knew that these things were true.

"Let God do what He knows is best," Eli whispered.

As time passed, people all over the land saw that Samuel honored God in all that he did. They saw also that God was with Samuel.

THINK

1. Think about the things God said about Eli's sons. Would you want God to say these things about you? 2. Now think about Samuel, and the way God helped him. Would you rather have God do this for you?

LEARN

From this story, you learn that you should show REVERENCE, or honor, to God.

DO

Find, or draw, a picture of a church, a Bible, and some people your age. Put these pictures in your room to remind you this week to honor, or reverence, God by going to His house, reading His Word, and telling your friends about Him.

Israel's First King

A Story about DECISION

"God has chosen you to be Israel's first king," Samuel said to Saul. Saul was surprised. He was a farmer, not a king. Only a few days ago he had left his father's home to search for some runaway donkeys. Someone thought the prophet Samuel could help him find the donkeys, so he came here to Samuel to ask. Now Samuel was telling Saul that he would be the next king of Israel!

Samuel took a jar of perfumed olive oil and poured it over Saul's head. This was called anointing. It showed that God wanted the man to be king. "Let God be with you," Samuel said. "Do whatever you decide is best, and He will not fail you."

Sometime later Samuel told the people of Israel to gather at Mizpeh. "You asked for a king," he said to them. "Now God has chosen a man named Saul to be your king." When Saul stood before the people, he was taller than anyone else in Israel. He certainly looked like he would make a good king. But would he be ready when the people needed him?

It wasn't long before the people did need him. A wicked king surrounded Jabesh, a city in Israel. "Let me gouge out every man's right eye," the king declared. "If you do not, I will destroy your city."

"Give us seven days to decide," replied the men of Jabesh. They sent messengers to Saul to tell him about their trouble. Saul remembered Samuel's words. He decided that he must fight this king. Quickly Saul gathered soldiers and during the night defeated the wicked king and his men.

The people were glad that day that Saul was their king. Saul knew that as long as he was close to God, God would help him make the right decisions.

THINK

1. How was Saul chosen to be king? 2. What did Saul do to show that he could make good decisions for God? 3. Every time you must choose something you must decide. Why should you ask God or parents to help you decide?

LEARN

From this story, you learn that you can decide the right way when God helps you. Ask Him!

DO

Draw a stoplight on a card. Put in a red light only. Draw a second one and put in the green light only. Put these up in your room to remind you to say yes (green light) to things that will please God and parents, and to say no (red light) to things that will not please them.

David is Chosen to be King

A Story about WISDOM

"I have chosen a new king for Israel," God told Samuel one day. "Saul was once a good king when he trusted Me to help him. But now Saul does not obey Me, so he cannot continue to be king."

Samuel listened to God. He knew that God's ways were wise. "Go to Bethlehem and see Jesse," God told Samuel. "I will show you which of his sons will become Israel's next king."

The people of Bethlehem were surprised to see the great prophet Samuel entering their small town. "Is there anything wrong?" the town leaders asked. "Everything is fine," Samuel replied. "We will have a feast together and worship God. Invite all the people."

Jesse and seven of his sons went to the feast. But David, the youngest, stayed home to watch the sheep. Samuel told Jesse that some day one of his sons would be the next king of Israel. Today God would show Samuel which son it would be.

Jesse asked his sons to walk before Samuel. The first and oldest was Eliab. Because he was tall and handsome, Samuel thought, "This must be the man God has chosen." But God said that He looks at a person's heart, not at his appearance. Each son stood before Samuel, but not one was the man God had chosen.

"Are these all the sons you have?" Samuel asked. "I have one more," Jesse said. "But he is just a boy, watching the sheep." Jesse sent for this boy David to come to Samuel.

When Samuel saw David coming, God told him that this was the one He had chosen to be Israel's next king. If Samuel could have looked into the future, he would have seen that God was making a wise choice. Samuel was glad that God sees things as they really are. Aren't you?

THINK

1. When Samuel looked at Jesse's oldest son, why did he think he would make a good king? Why was he wrong? What did God see? 2. Which is wiser, to look at someone's appearance, or to see his "heart," the way he really is? Why?

LEARN

From this story, you learn that it is wiser to see things as they really are, not as they appear to be. Good looks do not make a good heart.

DO

Pretend this week that each person you see is wearing a mask. Now try to get to know the person behind the mask. You may be surprised to find what a friend that person can be!

David and Goliath

A Story about TRUST

"Take some food to your brothers," Jesse told his son David one day. "And please find out if they are all right."

David wanted to fight in the army with his three older brothers. But he was the youngest, so he had to take care of the family sheep.

When David reached the camp he could tell that something was wrong and asked why. "See for yourself," said a soldier, pointing across the stream toward the Philistine camp.

There was the biggest man David had ever seen. "That is Goliath," the soldier said. "Listen to him!" Goliath walked to the edge of the stream and shouted at the Israelite army. "Send one man to fight me," he dared. "If I kill him, you must all become our slaves. If he kills me, we will become your slaves."

David was angry when he heard Goliath. "I will fight that giant myself," David cried. The soldiers heard David and took him to King Saul. "You can't do that!" the king said. "You are too young."

But David would not give up. "God helped me kill lions and bears when they attacked my sheep. And God will help me defeat this giant." Saul was amazed at the boy's trust in

God. So he sent him to fight Goliath.

David knelt by the stream and picked up five smooth stones. Then he went to meet Goliath. The giant laughed when he saw this young man. But David shouted, "You have a sword, a spear, and a shield on your side. But I have the God of heaven and earth on my side."

David slipped a stone into his sling-shot, whirled it around his head, and let the stone fly. It hit Goliath on the forehead and he dropped to the ground. That day the Israelite soldiers learned an important lesson. God helps those who trust Him.

THINK

1. Why were the soldiers of Israel afraid of Goliath? 2. Why wasn't David afraid of him? 3. How did David fight him? 4. Why do you think David won?

LEARN

From this story, you learn that God helps those who trust Him.

DO

Ask if this is right: A little person with big trust is bigger than a big person with little trust. What will you do about it?

Saul Tries to Kill David

A Story about LOYALTY

"Kill David!" Saul shouted at his son Jonathan and the palace attendants. Saul was afraid of David because God helped David in whatever he did. This made David famous and Saul jealous. Saul did not follow God anymore, so he wanted to kill David.

One day Saul was troubled. He needed some quiet music to calm him. David was a good musician, so he brought his harp into the palace to play for Saul. But still the king was not happy. Suddenly he hurled his spear at David. David ducked, then escaped from the palace. Saul and his men followed David all the way to Samuel's house in Ramah. There God stopped Saul from following David for awhile.

David hurried to find his best friend Jonathan. "I have always tried to be loyal to your father and please him," David explained. "So why is he trying to kill me? Now I must run away and hide."

Jonathan and David thought of a plan. "I will ask my father if he is really trying to kill you," Jonathan replied. "If he is, I will help you run away."

David hid by a field while Jonathan went to talk with King Saul. "You must leave at once," Jonathan said when he returned. "My father Saul wants to kill you." So David ran away into the wilderness. David could have fought Saul and become king. But David was loyal to Saul because God had made him king.

David found a cave in the hills and lived there. Other men came to live with David and made David their leader. When Saul learned that David was gone, he called together his best soldiers and hunted for David.

Saul kept looking for David whenever he could. Once Saul sat at the opening of a cave. He did not know that David was inside the cave. David could have killed Saul and become king. But he didn't. David knew that he would be king someday, but he wanted to let God decide the right time.

Once David crept into Saul's camp at night. While the king was sleeping, David took his spear and water jug. One of David's soldiers was going to kill Saul, but David stopped him.

As long as Saul lived, David served him faithfully because God had chosen Saul to be king. David was loyal to the one God had put in charge, and that made David loyal to God.

THINK

1. Why did Saul try to kill David? 2. What did David do? 3. Who has God put in charge of our lives? Why should we be loyal to them?

LEARN

From this story, you learn that you should be loyal to those God has placed over you.

DO

Ask three people who they are most loyal to. Then ask yourself the same question. Did any of them say parents? Did any say God? What does this tell you?

David Brings the Ark to Jerusalem

A Story about JOY

What a day this would be! King David had made plans to bring the Ark of the Covenant into Jerusalem, the capital city. It was about time! This beautiful golden chest had been in a man's home for many years. Now the king thought it should be in Jerusalem.

Everyone was excited when the king had the Ark put into an ox cart. The procession set out for Jerusalem in a happy mood. Then something happened. When one of the oxen stumbled, a man reached out to steady the Ark and keep it from falling. When he touched the Ark, he fell to the ground dead. King David was so sad. He had the Ark put in another home. Then he went back to Jerusalem.

During the next three months, David tried to find out what had happened. Then he knew. He had forgotten to look in God's Word to see how the Ark should be moved. He studied carefully what God said. He would move the Ark the way God wanted.

So David and his people set out again to move the Ark to Jerusalem. This time they did exactly what God said.

You should have heard the shouts of joy and the sounds of the trumpets. The air was filled with joy. But one person was not happy that day. King Saul's daughter Michal, who was also David's wife, was angry and jealous. When she looked from her window and saw David dancing with joy as he brought the Ark into the city, she hated him. And when he came home she began to argue with him about the way he danced in the streets with joy.

What a sad ending that was to a wonderful day. Michal was jealous and angry while everyone else was filled with joy.

But the Ark was where it should have been. King David placed it in a special tent and made many sacrifices to God. Then he gave food to every person who had come to share this wonderful day with him.

Most important, David's heart was full of joy that day because he had moved the Ark the way God wanted. That's the way to find joy in all that we do.

THINK

1. Why did things go wrong the first time the Ark was moved? 2. Why did things go right the next time? 3. Why was this such a day of joy?

LEARN

From this story, you learn that joy comes from doing things the way God wants them done.

DO

Cut out a round piece of cardboard like a big coin. One one side draw a smiling face. On the other side draw a sad face. When you do something that you think pleases God, put the smiling face up. When you do something you think does not please Him, put the sad face up. What will this remind you to do?

The Queen of Sheba Visits Solomon

A Story about WISDOM

"Who is this wise king?" the Queen of Sheba wondered. She had heard many stories of a great king named Solomon who had riches and wisdom beyond measure. "It is a long journey, but I must travel to Israel and see this man," the queen thought. "I must see how wise he really is."

After many days of travel, the tired queen entered the gates of Jerusalem where King Solomon lived. Following her was a camel caravan with the finest gifts her country had to offer.

King Solomon was waiting for the queen. He invited her into his splendid palace and showed her everything he had. When the Queen of Sheba saw the beautiful city, the storehouses full of gold, and the brilliant jewels, she could hardly speak.

The queen soon learned that Solomon was as wise as he was rich. She asked him every kind of difficult question, but the king always replied with a clear and simple answer.

The queen watched each day as King Solomon offered sweet-smelling sacrifices to God at the temple. The temple was the most magnificent building in the land of Israel, and Solomon had built it in worship and honor to the Lord.

At last it was time for the queen to go home. "Praise be to your God for making you king," she said to Solomon. That's what Solomon's people must have thought, too, for they were glad that God had given them such a wise king.

THINK

1. Who came to see King Solomon? Why did she come? 2. How did the queen know that Solomon was wise? 3. What did she say before she went home?

LEARN

From this story, you learn that Solomon was a wise king. That is because he had asked God to make him wise. Perhaps you should ask God to make you wise too.

DO

Read Proverbs 9:10. It tells you that you must love and respect the Lord before you can be wise. You will become wise as you read God's Word and pray to Him each day. Will you do that?

God Takes Care of Elijah

A Story about PROVIDING

"You are a wicked man," the prophet Elijah told King Ahab. "That is because you do not follow God. But God will show you how great He is. He will keep it from raining in Israel for a long time."

Ahab really was a wicked man. Since King Solomon died, many of Israel's kings would not follow God. Ahab was one of the worst. He prayed to idols of wood and stone. He even married Jezebel, a wicked woman who tried to kill those who worshiped God. But Elijah loved God and trusted Him to provide for him.

Ahab was angry at Elijah for stopping the rain. He wanted to hurt Elijah. So God told Elijah to hide.

Elijah found a little stream by the desert, where he had water to drink and a place to sleep. Ahab would not find him there. But what would Elijah eat? Elijah knew when he saw a big black raven flying toward him, bringing bread and meat in its bill. Each day the raven brought bread and meat for Elijah to eat. God had sent the raven to provide for Elijah.

At last the stream dried up and there was no water to drink. Even though it had not rained for a long time, Elijah knew that God would still take care of him. Then one day God told Elijah to go to the town of Zarephath. "There you will find a widow who will provide all the food and water you need," God said.

As Elijah entered the town gate, he saw the widow gathering sticks. "Please give me a drink of water and piece of bread," he asked her. "There is no bread left," the widow replied. "All that I have is a little jar of flour and a little jug of oil, just enough to make one last meal for myself and my son. When that is gone we will die."

"Don't be afraid," said Elijah. "God will provide for you the way He has provided for me." Then Elijah asked the widow to make a small biscuit of bread. "God says the jar of flour and the jug of oil will not become empty until it rains again in Israel," he told the widow.

Each day the widow used some flour from the jar and some oil from the jug. Each day there was enough to make bread for Elijah, the widow, and her son. Once again God provided!

THINK

1. How did God provide for Elijah by the stream? 2. How did God provide for Elijah at the widow's home? 3. How does God provide for you each day?

LEARN

From this story, you learn that God provides. He gives food and water and other things we need.

DO

Look in your refrigerator. What would Elijah and the widow have thought about the food in there? Why should you never complain about the things you don't have?

Elisha Raises a Boy to Life

A Story about KINDNESS

Imagine not having a Bible to read! In Elisha's day, the families in Israel did not have Bibles. They had only prophets to tell them about God. So Elisha walked around Israel, telling the people how to serve God.

One day Elisha entered the small town of Shunem. A kind woman ran out of her house and asked him to stay for a meal. After that, each time Elisha passed through Shunem, the woman and her husband invited Elisha to eat with them. Soon they became good friends.

"Let's build a small room on the roof for Elisha," the woman said to her husband one day. "Then Elisha can stay with us whenever he passes through town. And we can learn more about God."

Elisha was happy when the woman showed him his new room. Later he said to his servant Gehazi, "This woman has been so kind to us. What can we do to repay her for her kindness?" Gehazi had an idea. "This woman has always wanted a son," he replied. "But she has never had one." So Elisha talked to her.

"About this time next year you will hold your son in your arms," he promised. And just as Elisha had said, the next year God gave her a baby boy.

One day, when the child grew to be a strong boy, he was helping his father in the fields. Suddenly he became very sick and died. The woman of Shunem laid the boy on Elisha's bed. Then she saddled her donkey and rode away to find the prophet.

When she saw Elisha, she fell on her knees at his feet. "I never asked for a son because I was afraid something like this would happen," she cried. Elisha gave Gehazi his staff and said, "Run to the woman's house and lay the staff on the boy's face." Gehazi ran ahead and did what Elisha told him. But nothing happened.

Soon Elisha reached the house. He went into the room alone and prayed to God. Then he lay on top of the boy. Suddenly the boy sneezed and opened his eyes!

Elisha called the woman in. When she saw her son she cried with joy. She could not stop thanking Elisha. Once again Elisha had repaid the woman for her kindness.

THINK

1. How was the Shunammite couple kind to Elisha? 2. What did Elisha do for them? 3. Why should we be kind to others?

LEARN

From this story, you learn that you should always be kind to others. Sometime you may need their kindness in return.

DO

What is the most kind thing you have seen happen this week? What is the most unkind thing you have seen happen this week? Which do you think pleases God more? Why?

Naaman Is Healed

A Story about HUMILITY

Naaman was a very important man, the general of Syria's mighty army. But Naaman had one big problem. He was a leper, and there was no cure.

Naaman's little servant girl knew how he could get well. "Naaman can be healed if he goes to Israel and sees the great prophet," she said to his wife one day.

When Naaman heard about this prophet, he set out for Israel at once and went straight to the king. The king was frightened. "Am I God? How can I cure you?" he shouted. "Are you trying to start a fight with me?"

When the prophet Elisha heard about Naaman, he sent a message to the king. "Tell Naaman I am the man he wants to see."

Naaman jumped into his chariot and hurried to Elisha's house. "This man will do some great thing to heal me," Naaman thought as he ran to the door. But Elisha didn't even come out to see Naaman. He sent his servant instead. The servant opened the door and told Naaman, "Elisha says to wash seven times in the Jordan River and you will be healed.

Naaman stamped his foot with anger. "An important man like me should not have to wash in that dirty river," Naaman said. Then he started home. But his servants stopped him. "You want to get well, don't you?" they asked. Naaman thought about it. He was being too proud. He should do almost anything to get well, even wash in a dirty river. Do you know what happened when he stopped being proud and obeyed God's prophet? He was healed!

THINK

1. What was wrong with Naaman? Why did he go to see God's prophet? 2. What did Elisha tell Naaman to do? Why didn't Naaman want to do it? 3. What happened when Naaman stopped being proud and obeyed God's prophet? 4. Are you ever proud? Why is God pleased more when you are not proud?

LEARN

From this story, you learn that God can help you more when you stop being proud and let Him help you.

DO

Read 1 Peter 5:5-6. What does God do for those who are humble? Why not pray to God now, and ask Him to help you?

Jonah and the Big Fish

A Story about OBEDIENCE

"Jonah! Jonah!" Jonah sat up and listened as God spoke to him. "I have a special message for you," God said. "Go to the city of Nineveh. Tell the people that I will punish them because they do not obey Me."

Jonah was afraid to do what God said. Nineveh was one of the biggest cities in the world, in a country that did not like Israel. No wonder Jonah was frightened!

Jonah did not ask God to help him. Instead he ran away and boarded a large ship. But Jonah could not run away from God.

Out on the sea, a great storm hit and the ship was torn and battered by the winds. The sailors cried out to their gods, but of course they couldn't hear. Finally the sailors knew that Jonah was the cause of this storm. "Who are you, and what have you done to bring such trouble upon us?" they demanded.

"I am a prophet of the living God," Jonah replied. "My God is the Lord of the heaven and earth. He made the sea and dry land." Now the crew was even more afraid. "I have disobeyed God," Jonah said. "You must throw me overboard and save yourselves."

The ship was about to sink. So the sailors finally picked up Jonah and tossed him into the water. At once the sea became calm.

God sent a big fish to swallow Jonah. There in the belly of that fish Jonah learned his lesson and promised to obey God no matter what might happen to him. After three days and three nights, God spoke to the fish and it coughed Jonah up on dry land.

Jonah went straight to Nineveh to tell the people what God had said. The king listened to Jonah and was sorry for his sins. He commanded all the men and women of the city to set aside a special time to eat no food and to ask God to forgive their sins. When God saw that the people were truly sorry for the evil things they had done, He forgave them. Nineveh obeyed God and was not punished.

But Jonah wasn't happy. He thought Nineveh was so bad that God should destroy it. Jonah made a shelter outside the city and waited to see if God would change His mind. The sun grew hot, so God caused a vine to grow over Jonah's shelter to give him shade. Jonah was happy for the vine. But when the vine withered the next day, Jonah was angry that his shade was gone.

Then God spoke to Jonah. "You are concerned for this withered plant, even though you did not make it grow. Shouldn't I be

concerned about this great city with all its people? Until you came here with my message, they did not even know the difference between good and evil."

Now Jonah was sorry. When he was in the fish's belly, he had decided to obey God, and God had given him another chance. In the same way, God gave Nineveh a new chance to follow His ways.

THINK

1. Why was Jonah running away from God? 2. How did he learn to obey? 3. Why then did Jonah want Nineveh to be destroyed? 4. How did God teach him that Nineveh should be forgiven just as Jonah had been forgiven when he obeyed? 5. Who should you obey? Why?

LEARN

From this story, you learn that it is better to obey. You should obey God and your parents, shouldn't you?

DO

On a sheet of paper, write OBEY on the left side, and DISOBEY on the right. Under the word OBEY, write some things God or your parents want you to do. Under DISOBEY write some things they do not want you to do. Which side is better?

Isaiah Tells Others About God

A Story about PROMISES

God wanted to do great things for His people. He gave them many wonderful promises. All they had to do was obey. That is why God sent prophets. The prophets told the people about God's promises. They taught the people how to please God and believe in His promises.

One day a man named Isaiah had a dream. In the dream God called him to be a prophet. "Isaiah," God said. "Listen to Me. Tell the people what I am about to say."

Then God began. "Long ago I promised Abraham that all the nations of the earth would one day receive My most wonderful gift. But that gift would come only through Jesus, My Son. The gift is eternal life and forgiveness for sin instead of punishment."

Isaiah told the people about God's promise that Jesus would come some day. "Please stop following idols," Isaiah begged the people. "And listen to the wonderful things God wants to do for you."

Isaiah believed God with all his heart. He believed God so much that he couldn't stop telling the people about God's goodness. It did not matter who Isaiah was talking to. It did not matter how many people made fun of him. Isaiah would never stop telling others about God and His wonderful promises.

THINK

1. What did God promise to Abraham? 2. What special gift did God promise to His people? 3. What book has many of God's promises for you to read? Why should you read it each day and believe God's promises?

LEARN

From this story, you learn that God has many wonderful promises, and that He keeps each of them.

DO

Read Isaiah 53 together as a family. As you do, picture the crucifixion of Jesus. Isaiah was telling God's promise to send Jesus to die for our sins.

Hezekiah Pleases God

A Story about PRAYER

"King Hezekiah!" a servant shouted. "A big army is marching toward our city." Hezekiah looked. It was the army of Assyria, the strongest army in the world.

Soon a messenger came to the gates of Jerusalem. He was from the king of Assyria. "The king says that you should give up now," he told Hezekiah. "You cannot fight against us." The people of Jerusalem listened to the messenger. They were afraid. But Hezekiah said to them, "Don't be afraid. You must trust God."

Again the king of Assyria sent a messenger to Jerusalem. This time he brought a letter. Hezekiah read the letter. It said, "Hezekiah, do not trust your God to save you. I have captured many cities as big as Jerusalem. Their gods did not save them, so why do you think your God will help you? Give up now and you will be spared."

Hezekiah took the king's letter to the temple. He spread it out before God. Then Hezekiah prayed, "O Lord, the king of Assyria says that You cannot save Jerusalem. Please save us and show the Assyrians that you are the God of the whole earth."

That night God sent an angel into the army camp of Assyria. The angel killed so many soldiers that the rest ran away. God had answered Hezekiah's prayer.

Many years later Hezekiah became sick. "Soon you will die," the prophet Isaiah told him. Hezekiah was sad. "O Lord," he prayed as he lay in bed, "I have been faithful to you all of my life. I have taught the people to love You. Please do not let me die yet."

Hezekiah did not die. Once again God answered Hezekiah's prayer because he was a good king. Hezekiah was thankful that God was his friend.

THINK

1. When the king of Assyria came, what did Hezekiah ask God to do? What did God do?
2. When Hezekiah got sick, what did he ask God to do? What did God do? 3. When you need help, who should you ask to help you? Why should you pray, instead of doing what you please?

LEARN

From this story, you learn that God listens to your prayers.

DO

God always listens to your prayers. He has three answers: no, yes, and wait. The next time you pray, see which answer God sends. Write PRAY on a card and put it on the door of your room. It will remind you to pray before you leave your room.

Into the Fiery Furnace

A Story about COURAGE

"I am such a great king," proud Nebuchadnezzar thought to himself. "I will build a large golden statue of myself. All of the royal officials from across my kingdom must come and worship it."

Soon the king's servants were busy making the king's statue of gold. At last the big day arrived. A servant read the king's order. "When the musicians play their instruments," he read, "everyone must bow down and worship the golden statue. Anyone who does not will be thrown into a furnace of fire."

The crowd became quiet. The musicians began to play, and everyone bowed low before the statue—everyone but Shadrach, Meshach, and Abednego.

Nebuchadnezzar was both angry and sad. He liked Shadrach, Meshach, and Abednego. They were such good and honest men that Nebuchadnezzar had promoted them to high positions within his kingdom.

"Why did you not obey my order?" the king shouted. "Do you want to be thrown into the fiery furnace?"

"God is able to save us if He wants to," the men began. "But even if He doesn't save us, we will serve only the true God." What a courageous thing to say!

King Nebuchadnezzar was angry now. At his command, the soldiers threw Shadrach, Meshach, and Abednego into the blazing furnace.

But Nebuchadnezzar could not believe his eyes. Now there were four men in the furnace, and one looked like an angel! "Come out of there," yelled the king. Shadrach, Meshach, and Abednego walked safely out of the fire. Not even their clothes were burned.

"Praise the God of Shadrach, Meshach, and Abednego," the king exclaimed. "These men trust their God and do what they know is right, even when others try to stop them."

THINK

1. Why didn't the three friends bow down before the golden statue? 2. What did the king do to them? 3. How did these three men show that they had courage to obey God? 4. Do you have the courage to do what God wants? 5. Do you have the courage to tell your friends that you love God?

LEARN

From this story, you learn that God helps those who show courage to do what He wants.

DO

Read Deuteronomy 31:6. What does this tell you about showing courage for God? Would you like to memorize this verse?

Daniel in the Lion's Den

A Story about PRAYER

"We must catch Daniel doing something wrong," some bad men said. "Then the king will have to get rid of him." But the men could find nothing wrong with Daniel. These men hated Daniel because Darius, the new king, had just made Daniel the second most important man in the kingdom. They wanted to have Daniel's job. They would even kill him to get it.

The bad men thought of a plan. "Daniel is too good," they said. "We will never catch him doing something wrong. Let's make a law that says that everyone must pray to the king only for 30 days." The men knew that Daniel prayed to God every morning, noon, and night. And they knew that Daniel would never stop praying. Daniel loved God too much.

The men went to Darius. They bragged about him and made him feel important. Then they talked him into making the new law.

One day the men caught Daniel praying to God as usual. "Daniel is not obeying your new law," they said to the king. The king was sorry now that he had made the law. He liked Daniel and did not want to kill him. But he could not change the law. "I hope that your God, to whom you pray, will rescue you," he told Daniel. Then the men threw Daniel into a den of hungry lions.

King Darius could not sleep that night. Early in the morning he ran to the lions' den. "Daniel!" he called out. "Was your God able to save you?" The king was overjoyed when he heard Daniel's voice. God had shut the mouths of the hungry lions so Daniel was saved.

The king's men took Daniel out of the lions' den. Darius took the evil men who had tried to get Daniel killed and threw them into the lions' den. Then he made a newer law which said that everyone should honor God, for He was the true God.

THINK

1. Why did the evil men want to hurt Daniel? 2. How did they plan to get him killed? 3. Why do you think Daniel would not stop praying? 4. Why should you keep on praying each day? Do you?

LEARN

From this story, you learn that it is a good idea to keep on praying to God each day, no matter what happens.

DO

Ask God to help you remember to pray. Ask your parents also to help you remember to pray.

Queen Esther Saves Her People

A Story about COURAGE

"Who is the most beautiful young woman in my kingdom?" King Ahasuerus wondered. The king wanted to find a new queen, so he sent his servants to bring many beautiful women to see him. He would choose one to be his queen.

One of the young women was a Jewish girl named Esther. Her uncle Mordecai took care of her. When the king decided to make Esther his queen, Mordecai came to the palace gate to hear news about her.

Each morning a wicked man named Haman rode through the palace gate. He was a very important man, so people bowed down before him. But Mordecai would not bow down. He believed that he should bow down only to God.

Haman was furious. He made plans to have all of the Jewish people in the land killed. He knew that included Mordecai, but he did not know that it included Queen Esther.

Mordecai learned about Haman's evil plan. He told Queen Esther she must do something about it. But what? Esther could not even go to see the king without being asked. If she did, the king could kill her for doing it.

Esther wondered what she should do.

Then she decided. She would go to see the king. That was a very brave thing to do. Esther knew she was risking her life to save her people.

When the king saw Esther, he held out his golden scepter. That told her that he would not kill her. Instead, he listened to her. Then the king stopped the wicked Haman from killing Queen Esther, Mordecai and their people. Now Esther was glad that she had the courage to go to the king.

THINK

1. Why did Haman want to kill Mordecai and his people? 2. How did Esther stop him? 3. How did Esther show that she had courage? 4. What are some ways you can show courage to do what God wants?

LEARN

From this story, you learn that Esther had courage and saved her people. Showing courage may help you please God more, or help someone know Him better. That's worth doing, isn't it?

DO

Choose the words that you think relate to Esther: COURAGE, AFRAID, BRAVE, COWARD, TIMID, WEAK, UNAFRAID.

IMPORTANT VALUES TAUGHT IN THIS BOOK

COURAGE, Stories 27, 44, 46
DECISION, Story 32
DEDICATION, Story 25
FAITHFULNESS, Stories 13, 29
FORGIVENESS, Story 15
HAPPINESS, Story 2
HONESTY, Story 10
HUMILITY, Stories 14, 40
JEALOUSY, Stories 4, 12
JOY, Story 36
KINDNESS, Stories 24, 39
LOVE, Stories 11, 30
LOYALTY, Story 35
OBEDIENCE, Stories 5, 7, 17, 19, 22, 26, 41
ORDERLINESS, Story 1
POWER, Story 18
PRAYER, Stories 43, 45
PROMISES, Stories 6, 42
PROVIDING, Stories 8, 16, 21, 38
REVERENCE, Story 31
SELF-CONTROL, Story 28
TEMPTATION, Story 3
TRUST, Stories 9, 20, 23, 34
WISDOM, Stories 33, 37